A Flight
to Elsewhere

A Flight to Elsewhere

Samuel Hazo

PS3515.A9877 F58 2005
Hazo, Samuel John.
A flight to elsewhere
Pittsburgh : Autumn House
Press, c2005.

Autumn House Press

PITTSBURGH

"Autumn House" and "Autumn House Press" are registered trademarks owned by Autumn House Press, a non-profit corporation whose mission is the publication and promotion of poetry.

Text and cover design: Kathy Boykowycz
Cover photo: William Albert Allard

Autumn House Press Staff
Executive Director: Michael Simms
Director of Development: Susan Hutton
Community Outreach Director: Michael Wurster
Assistant Editor: Jack Wolford
Editorial Consultant: Eva Simms
Media Consultant: Jan Beatty
Marketing Consultant: Matt Hamman

ISBN: 1-932870-04-0
Library of Congress: 2004113774

Printed in the U.S.A. by Thomson-Shore of Dexter, Michigan
All Autumn House books are printed on acid-free paper and meet the international standards of permanent books intended for purchase by libraries.

The Autumn House Poetry Series

Michael Simms, editor

Snow White Horses, Selected Poems 1973-1988
   by Ed Ochester
The Leaving, New and Selected Poems by Sue Ellen Thompson
Dirt by Jo McDougall
Fire in the Orchard by Gary Margolis
Just Once, New and Previous Poems by Samuel Hazo
The White Calf Kicks by Deborah Slicer
   (Winner of the 2003 Autumn House Poetry Prize, selected by
   Naomi Shihab Nye)
The Divine Salt by Peter Blair
The Dark Takes Aim by Julie Suk
Satisfied with Havoc by Jo McDougall
Half Lives, Petrarchan Poems by Richard Jackson
Not God After All by Gerald Stern
   with drawings by Sheba Sharrow
Dear Good Naked Morning by Ruth L. Schwartz
   (Winner of the 2004 Autumn House Poetry Prize, selected by
   Alicia Ostriker)
A Flight to Elsewhere by Samuel Hazo

Other Works by Samuel Hazo

Poetry
Just Once
As They Sail
The Holy Surprise of Right Now
The Past Won't Stay
   Behind You
Silence Spoken Here
Nightwords
The Color of Reluctance
Thank a Bored Angel
To Paris
Quartered
Once for the Last Bandit
Twelve Poems
Blood Rights
My Sons in God
Listen with the Eye
The Quiet Wars
Discovery

Fiction
Stills
The Wanton Summer Air
The Very Fall of the Sun
Inscripts

Criticism
Smithereened Apart:
   A Critique of Hart Crane
The Autobiographers of
   Everybody

Essays
The Pittsburgh That Stays
   Within You
The Feast of Icarus
The Rest Is Prose
Spying for God

Plays
Feather
Solos
Until I'm Not Here Anymore
Mano a Mano:
   A Flamenco Drama
   (The Life of Manolete)
Watching Fire, Watching Rain

Translations
The Pages of Day and Night
   (Poems of Adonis)
Lebanon: Twenty Poems for
   One Love
   (Poems of Nadia Tueni)
Transformations of the Lover
   (Poems of Adonis)
The Growl of Deeper Waters
   (Essays of Denis de
   Rougemont)
The Blood of Adonis

Chapbooks
Jots before Sleep
Ballads and Duets
Latching the Fist
Shuffle, Cut and Look

Acknowledgments

Some of the poems in this collection have appeared in *The American Scholar, The Atlantic Monthly, Commonweal, Hawaii Pacific Review, The Hudson Review, Janus Head, Mystique, New Letters, Notre Dame Magazine, Notre Dame Review, Pittsburgh Post-Gazette, River Walk Journal, Salmagundi, Shenandoah, Stand, The Worcester Review,* and *Tar River Poetry.*

I would like to thank William Albert Allard for permission to use his memorable photograph on the jacket.

Contents

The Mutineer   1

1

Ongoing Presences Have No Past Tense   5
The Kiss   7
American Games   8
What Lasts Lasts   11
Mustangs   13
Order of Battle   14
Notre Dame du Lac   15
The Wreck   19
National Prayer Breakfast   20
How Married People Break and Make Up   22
The Wounds of Honor   26
Welcome to New York   28
Away   31

2

Filling My Pen for Action   35
The Power of Less   37
Documentation   38
Manolete and Islero   40
Sex   41
The General   43
Accident Ahead   44
Seeing My Mother in My Grandson   46
On the Stroke of   47
The View from Above   50
Middlemost   52
Everything   54
In the Time of the Tumult of Nations   56

3

Encore, Encore   61
At Home   63
For Which It Stands   65
The Nearness That Is All   67
Paring Pairs of Pears   69
Body Language   70
My Shirt Inspector Reassures Me   73
At Churchill's Grave   75
Tortoise Time   77
Towels   78
Woman with Walker and
  Limping Dog   80
Lucky   81
For Anna Catherine at
  Thanksgiving   83

4

A Czech Susannah in Cannes   87
There's Such a Thing As
  Lightning   89
Novembering   91
Resoundings   92
Such Stuff   93
Crisscross   95
The Slower the Surer   96
Passing Through   98
A New Deal   99
Senior Moments   102
Mediterranean Update   104
Ballad of All Battles   106
Do You Read Me?   107

5

Academia Supremia Anemia   111
Going with the Flow   113
Seesaws   115
Hugh   116
"Wanted: Meaningful Overnight
  Partner"   118
Amazement This Way Lies   119
RSVP   121
Facing Winter   123
The Situation   125
None But the Brazen   127
What's Left   128
The Necessary Brevity of
  Pleasures   130
To Be   132

For Mary Anne
Then, now, still, ever

The Mutineer

Leaves curl against the ground
  like Muslims at prayer.
                        In weeks
  they'll change from elegies in place
   into their own obituaries.
                         Now
  they leave me leafing back,
  back, back.
             My father meets me
  on the way.
             At eighty he told me
  he was shrinking.
               Lately, I've felt
  the same, not physically, but otherwise.
The more I add the sum of all
  the living to the once alive,
  the more I seem to vanish
  in the balance.
              Watching the way
  of leaves prefigures what I know
  will come.
          It urges me
  to take a flight to elsewhere
  or make my creed defiance.
Meantime, I choose to mount
  my mutiny in words…
                  Not much
  as protests go, but something.

1

Ongoing Presences Have No Past Tense

I keep whatever stays as intimate
  as breath and, like all breathing,
  of the instant: my father's aftershave,
  the whiteness of his shirts, his hair
  still black at eighty-two,
  the hats he always wore brim up,
  the eyes of Cynthia gone sullen
  with desire, supper in Geneva
  when a waiter in tuxedo boned
  the lemon sole as deftly as a surgeon
  operating on an eye, the day
  of Kennedy's murder when all
  the clocks struck nil and stayed there,
  my last goodbye to Jane
  and how we sensed it as we spoke.
Compared to these, who cares
  if Candidate Twice and Candidate Once
  insult the day with presidential
  dreams?
        For them today's
a preface, nothing more.
             The same
holds true for all who bet
on dynasties, prognostications, jackpots
or the gold of fools.
          I trust
the body's unforgettable assurances
that know what's true without
discussion or hypocrisy.

                        The teeth
     with just one bite can tell
     an apple from a pear.
                        The tongue
     can savor at a touch what's salt,
     what's sugar.
                    Balsam and skunk
       cannot confuse the nose.
Even in darkness the hand
       knows silk from gabardine.
Whatever makes a sound and what
       resounds when sound evaporates
       is music to the ear.
                        The eye
       does not discriminate, and everything
       in its complete democracy is ours
       in perpetuity to keep as near
       as here and dearer than now.

The Kiss

While the river turned and slid
  under a gray bridge that cars
  kept crossing on their way
  to Michigan, and somewhere a band
  was blaring a march by Sousa,
  she eased her lips around
  his lips so firmly that the musk
  that rises in the body of a girl
  aroused was his to taste.
In time, when she no longer
  was the mystery for him she used
  to be, the echo of the ichor
  of that kiss could resurrect the grayness
  of the bridge, the spurting cars,
  the river, and the drums of Sousa,
  and then, arising like a swimmer
  from the depth of half a century,
  the very face and figure
  of a girl whose mouth sealed his
  so tightly that their top-teeth ticked
  like a kiss gone bumpy
  though the kiss went on and on,
  and when it stopped, the band
  had marched to sleep, the bridge
  was empty, and the sliding river
  sailored south without a sound.

American Games

"Games are human activities made difficult for the joy of it."
   John Ciardi

"No one can take away from a man what he has done with his
hands and his feet."
   From the Ancient Greek

Viewed from above, a tennis
   court's rectangular.
                              Add
   lanes on either side for doubles.
Clearing the net for diagonal
   serves, a server's allowed
   a hand's spread of space.
To keep the ball in play
   in bounds is all that tennis
   means…
                    A basketball
   seems tamed in the hands
   of the best dribblers.
                              But dribbling's
   just the calisthenics of the game.
The purpose is to score
   repeatedly.
                    Hoopshots obey
   the laws of physics.
                              Simply
   by shooting, the best shooters
   can gauge if the hoop's too low
   or high by fractions of inches…
Baseball's Odyssean.
                    To start

from home and then return
is all that counts.
                        Some runners
die en route on first,
second or third.
                        Home runs
disrupt the game.
                        Odysseus
trots before the saga
starts again.
                        Cyclopean
pitchers' wiles, the Siren
skills of infielders and outfielders,
the Lotosland of walks
or the Scylla and Charybdis
of rundowns await each batter…
Football's a warfare of ground
   troops and air but basically
   Napoleonic – force against weakness,
   adjusted attacks, deceptions,
   the blunder of fumbles at scrimmage.
It all comes down to yards
   lost or yards gained – digits
   on a scoreboard.
                        When it's over,
   it's over…
                        Generations have played
   these games to make them theirs.
Plantagenet's racquets are Spaulding's
   now.

The two-handed set's
become a dunk.
The Babe's
fifty-four ounce bat's
been slimmed to thirty-six.
The shape of this year's football
makes the former dropkick
obsolete.
But still it's play,
despite the dollar signs,
the deals, the coastal schedules,
and the irony of watching men
engaged in boys' games
for tycoon's wages.
Some say
it's pastime, merely pastime –
brief and seasonal and mock-heroic.
Pastime or not, it shows
the body at its most athletic.
Unexpectedly, a lone player
may accomplish something
no one's done before.
It lasts
in three-point type in the records –
a blink against oblivion.

What Lasts Lasts

On his left wrist, Vassilikos
    wore twin watches – one
    his own, the other his dead
    wife's.
                Side by side
    and synchronized, they kept
    identical time.
                        Need I
    elaborate?
                    But then who shuns
    what contradicts absentia?
Calling my wife in Pittsburgh
    from New Hampshire, we mock
    geography with words since we
    feel nearer on the phone than when
    we're near enough to talk....
What makes the book I wrote
    three years ago seem dearer
    than the last?
                    Like any outgrown
    photograph it tells me how
    I used to be and tracks me
    like my shadow....
                        Even
    my sacred blunders hate
    to abdicate: the famous man
    I introduced by the wrong name,
    the trip I never should have made,
    the day I swam out farther
    than I should and barely made it back....

Last night I read a pair
   of bumper stickers on a Subaru's
   backside: "We are the people
   our parents warned us about" –
   "God is coming, and She's
   mad."
            Of all I've seen
   and heard since then, what makes me
   keep in mind those two, those two?

Mustangs
5th Special Basic Class, U. S. Marine Corps

Older by fifty years,
   we grouped for photographs beside
   apartment BOQ's that once
   were Quonset huts.
                    The new
   lieutenants held us in embarrassing
   esteem.
            Of some three hundred
   in our old battalion, three
   were killed in combat, and the rest
   lived on to die of the usual
   or simply to survive and re-unite.
Necklaced with name-cards to prove
   we were who we were, we met
   without bravado.
                    Grandfathers mostly,
   we drank black coffee like alumni
   and avoided politics.
                    Two days
   together placed us squarely
   in our generation.
                    No one pretended
   to be other than himself.
                    We parted
   as we parted half a century
   before, uncertain when or where
   we'd meet again.
            Or if.

Order of Battle

Trappers say traps are truly
  traps when no one thinks
  they are: spiked pits covered
  with fronds, a saw-toothed jaw
  levered to snap at a touch,
  the smile that lulls the victim
  while the rapist bides his time.
Unlike attackers, trappers
  wait and wait until escape's
  impossible.
                Their onslaught
  happens suddenly from all
  directions in a pure deception
  where the doomed awake too late…
To schedule strategies where strength
  exploits a weakness, shrewd
  attackers plan by the clock.
Timing – timing is all.
Some say there's something
  in this ratio that's sexual.
Considering the ways of animals,
  that's true: entrapment
  after thrust, bait against bite,
  uncountable scenarios of ambush
  and assault, stealth versus guile.

Notre Dame du Lac

1

Everywhere the same campus trees –
   fifty autumns thicker, taller
   and scheduled to sleeve their naked
   bark in January's ermine.
A male and female cardinal
   peck at huckleberries on a limb.
Paired for life, they beak
   each berry as their last and first.
Sparrows cling to branches,
   wires, sheer brick walls,
   anything where they can roost.
A chipmunk scoots and pauses
   by the numbers.
                    Unlike all peacock
   prancers on parade or the zombie
   stomp of soldiery, backpacking
   students cycle, rollerblade
   or stroll to their different drummers.
They pass like Giacometti's
   striders – eyes full front
   but aimed at destinations still
   within themselves…
                    Beyond
   Nantucket a jet's about to crash.
Bradley's challenging Gore.
Ted Hesburgh's fit and eighty-two
   with one good eye.
                    "May I
   serve God better with one eye
   than I did with two."

                                        Seated
                behind me at the football game,
                a woman from Dallas tells me
                her Pittsburgh mother had an uncle –
                Leo O'Donnell, a doctor.
                                        She knows
                I've flown from Pittsburgh for the game.
                Eighty thousand cheer around us.
                "O'Donnell!" she repeats.
                                        I swallow
                and say that Dr. O'Donnell funded
                "my scholarship to study here"
                a half-century ago.
                                        The odds
                are eighty thousand plus to one
                that I should meet his Texas niece
                today in this jammed stadium
                in Indiana, but I do.
                                        What else
                is there to say?
                                        It's now
                all over the world.
                                        Everything's
                happening.
                                        Anything can happen.

        2

We've journeyed back to grass
   and souvenirs and beige bricks.
The sky's exactly the same.

Acre by acre, the campus
  widens like a stage designed
  for a new play.
                Why
do we gawk like foreigners
at residence halls no longer
ours but somehow ours
in perpetuity?
              We visit them
like their alumni – older
but unchanged.
                Half a century
of students intervenes.
                  They stroll
among us now, invisible
but present as the air before
they fade and disappear.
                  It's like
the day we swam St. Joseph's
Lake.
      We churned the surface
  into suds with every stroke and kick.
After we crossed, the water
  stilled and settled to a sheen
  as if we never swam at all.
One memory was all we kept
  to prove we'd been together
  in that very lake, and swimming.
Each time we tell this story,
  someone says we're living out
  a dream.

We say we're only
reuniting with the lives
we lived.
As long as we
can say they were, they *were*…
And what they were, we are.

The Wreck

Three wheels of the overturned
  truck are stopped while the fourth
  keeps turning, doing its job
  as if the air were now the road.
And there's the parked Plymouth,
  its hood and headlights bulldogged
  by the impact.
              A cracked telephone
  pole dangles snapped and sizzling
  wires.
       Gasoline smears
  its rainbow, curb to curb.
Thrown clear, the driver cowers
  on the berm, curled up, crying,
  rattled but unhurt.
            His cigarettes
  and bills of lading in the blazing
  cab incinerate in silence.
              Sirens
  announce an ambulance, firetrucks,
  trios of police cars.
          Gawkers
  snoop like extras on a movie
  set whose only role is
  always to be in the way.
By morning nothing will remain
  but peelings of tire rubber burned
  into a skidmark.
           That, and a man's
  black shoe, its lace still tied.

National Prayer Breakfast

Conventioneers from thirty-seven
  countries throng the banquet
  hall to hear the message.
A clergyman asks God to bless
  the fruit and rolls.
                The President
  speaks up for Reagan, Martin
  Luther King and having faith
  in faith.
          Love is the common
  theme, most of it touching,
  all of it frank, unburdening
  and lengthy.
            If faith is saying so,
  then this is faith.
            The problem is
  that I must be the problem.
I've always thought that faith
  declaimed too publicly destroys
  the mystery.
             Years back,
  when Brother Antoninus yelled
  at listeners to hear the voice
  of Jesus in them, Maura said,
  "The Jesus in me doesn't talk
  that way."
          Later, when I saw
  a placard bannering, "Honk,
  if you love Jesus," I thought
  of Maura's words and passed
  in silence…

                    Jesus in fact
        spoke Aramaic in Jerusalem,
        foretold uninterrupted life
        and sealed it with a resurrection.
If He asked me to honk
        in praise of that, I'd honk
        all day.
                    But rising from the dead
        for me seems honk enough
        since no one's done it since,
        and no one did it earlier or ever.
Others might disagree, and that's
        their right.
                    But there's an inner
        voice I hear that's one
        on one and never out of date.
It's strongest when it's most subdued.
I'll take my Jesus straight.

How Married People Break and Make Up

1

He said, "I'm not ignoring you."
She called him a name.
                    He mumbled
  what she thought she heard.
"And don't say a word about
  my mother, you snob."
                    He held
  a single scrubbed potato
  in his hand and said, "I asked you
  for another, and your mother
  had nothing to do with it."
"Don't lie."
              He denied whatever
  she denied whenever she denied
  whatever he denied.
                    Meanwhile
  the dog hid in the pantry.
"You think more of the dog
  than you think of me!"
                    With that
  she marched upstairs and shut
  the bedroom door with a will.
When she returned to the kitchen,
  she was dressed for the street.
"I'm going to my sister's, so don't
  wait for me."
              "Dinner's
  on the table."
                    "I hope you enjoy it."

"Remember Ernie Cavanaugh?"
She started to leave, then turned.
"What about Ernie Cavanaugh?"
"What about who?"
                    "Ernie
   Cavanaugh – you brought it up!"
"I saw him at lunch with his wife,
   that's all, and they looked great."
"He couldn't look great because
   he's still in love with me."
"I doubt if anyone could stop
   being in love with you."
"Who is she?"
                    "She said her name
   was Gretchen."
                    "Gretchen?"
                              "Gretchen."
"Did Ernie ask about me?"
"So many times he made me think
   you married the wrong man."
"Don't ever say that."
                    "Maybe
   it's true."
              "I'd never marry
   a man with dirty fingernails,
   and Ernie had dirty fingernails."
"I thought you were going to Ruth's."
"I changed my mind," she said
   as she sat across from him
   and added, "I can change my mind
   whenever I want to, can't I?"

2

"Sometimes you tune me out."
He stopped reading and smiled
   at her, "Why would I do that?"
"I don't know why, but you do."
"I like to think that I listen
   carefully, especially to you."
"You listen, but you don't hear me."
He tried to name what lurked
   behind her words: frustration,
   boredom, envy?
                                    At times
   like this he thought not answering
   was best.
                       "That's typical of you,"
   she smirked, "to say nothing or leave
   the room."
                             "What's wrong with that?"
"It's what men do, but women
   know that one of Shakespeare's
   ladies said it best – 'I'm
   a woman – what I think
   I say.'"
                       "I say what *I* think."
"Two days later."
                                    "Better
   late than..."
                             He knew her mood
   would make her say she had
   to get away, that anywhere

was better than here, that what
she had was nil compared
to what she lacked.
                              "Kenny
and Rose are always going
out or away somewhere,"
she said, "but you stay put
right here."
                    "Right here is where
we live, remember?"
                          "But you
do nothing to change the tempo,
and every woman likes surprises."
"Finding you was the best surprise
of my life, Marie, and I
love you for who you are,
not what you do or where
you want to go."
                        She turned
away to keep the tears
from showing, but the tears kept
coming when she said,"You always
do that."
              "Do what?"
                              He offered
her his handkerchief.
                              Accepting it,
she said, "You always say something
that makes me cry when all
I wanted was a good, old-fashioned fight."

The Wounds of Honor

Stroke victims and Alzheimer's
   shut-ins forget what's happening
   as totally as they forgot what happened.
Some say it's partially a blessing
   to be spared the frowns of recollection.
I have my doubts since nothing
   but the past assures us that today
   without a yesterday is life
   without a link.
                       What else but memory
   restores the dead?
                       And what's experience
   but what's remembered as we go?
And where but in the minds of exiles
   do their countries stay alive?
Nothing but knowing what we know
   enlivens us to meet the envy
   of the never satisfied, the wiles
   of the ravenous for glory or the jealousy
   of those imprisoned by their own
   abundance.
                       Between the mind
   reflective and the mind presumptive
   waits the mind attentive and composed.
It says who learns from history
   grows wise through disappointment.
It says who trusts in prophecy
   deserves the folly of his dreams.
Sentenced to be sage, we learn
   that life means living with conditions
   as they are.

But those who roam
the limbo of amnesia travel free
of consequence like astronauts released
by gravity to sail unfettered
for a star.
　　　　They age unwounded
by remembrances while we recall
our far from unforgotten wars
in unforgettable detail.
　　　　　　　　Each battle
was a struggle.
　　　　　　Each struggle taught
a lesson.
　　　　Each lesson left a scar.

Welcome to New York

1

My sparrow preens in a fountain
  pool that mirrors the World
  Trade Center upside down.
She fluffs and shudders dry
  like a dog after a dousing.
                              What's
  a sparrow or its fall to world trade?
On a scale of one to ten
  she fails to quantify.
                              Like all
  the lilliputians of this world
  she struts her two cents' worth
  of insignificance and wants no more
  than to be seen.
                              Since no one
  notices what's small unless it turns
  into a threat, Gullivers stroll by
  and overlook my sparrow.
                              She pecks
  a battered apple scattered
  near a bench I've commandeered.
I've come out here to smoke
  my pipe.
                              Since smoking is forbidden
  in New York except in "designated
  areas," I greet my fellow outcast
  in the free and unforbidden air.
                              And there
  we stay, undesignated as we are.

Banished from Eden to a concrete
  park, we're seen as two
  of a dangerous type – Eve
  on a spree with her little Big Apple,
  Adam at peace with his pipe.

June 24, 2001

  2

In just one year we've traveled
  from the flying snow of faxes,
  memoranda, jiffy notes –
  clouds of spume the color
  of gun-metal and swirled
  to the sun in volleys of smoke –
  cartwheeling bodies flailing
  by sealed or shattered windows
  to battering, smattering rest –
  a mayor masked on scene
  but busily a mayor – firefighters
  by the hundreds shouldering
  flattened hoses coiled
  like bandoleers – policemen
  with sooted lips and foreheads –
  funerals for thousands crushed
  to sift – re-runs of tons
  of aircraft penetrating steel
  and glass until the targets
  buckled slowly to their knees
  like bison gutshot as they stood –

to something excavated
like an open grave, then "Patriotic
Travel Mugs" and "God-Bless-
America Hotel Discounts"
and "NYPD Authentic Caps"
and "Lapel Flags Priced
from $9.99 to $99.99
with Genuine Diamond Settings."

September 11, 2002

Away

I'm in Pennsylvania.
                        You're
in Asia Minor.
                    The echo
of your voice from the next room,
your palm against my shoulder
and your way of looking at a lily
sleep together like your nightgowns
in a drawer.
                    Somehow we know
a deeper closeness, but the price
is distance.
                Or is it simply time
away regardless of the miles?
Last night I woke up shattered
  by the voice of someone at the pitch
  of panic from a nightmare,
  and the voice was mine.
                            Against
real fears, especially in dreams,
there's no defense.
                        I fear
for you despite myself.
                            I fear
for me without you.
                        Nothing
distracts me but distraction.
Separately ourselves we're still
  each other's while the hemispheres
  between us keep us more
  together than apart but still
  apart.
            I hate these merciless

nights that madden me with all
that could go wrong.
                    I miss
the sight and sound and touch
of you.
          I need you near enough
to hold.
            I need you here.

Filling My Pen for Action

I thumb the plunger down
  and siphon black ink up
  the way a hypodermic needle
  siphons plasma from a vein.
My ink of choice is ebony
  because it promises to last.
But last as what?
                          Notations,
  doodles, letters, labels,
  numbers, signatures on checks
  or shopping lists?
                          History's
  no guide.
                    Our circumstances
  change.
                    Regardless, writing
  what we think makes thinking
  truer when we see it written down.
The bravest pages of a poem
  or a book began as blanks
  that craved the consecration of a pen.
And written words increase
  in value over time.
                              Shakespeare's
  one surviving letter (a request
  for money from a lord) now seems
  as holy as the hairlock of a saint.
The same applies to Jefferson's
  handwritten declaration, Whitman's
  jottings, and (for me) my mother's
  letters in a hatbox or my aunt's
  last sentence on an index card....

Recalling this, I watch my nib
  change ink-blood into words
  across this very page to show
  why every word should be as sacred
  as the final word I'll write.

The Power of Less

Dead lives commemorated
   on a coin or crammed into a book
   or briefly mentioned in a footnote....
Is it all a matter of shrinkage?
The way of the world, you say,
   the way of entropy or wine,
   the way the body ages
   into something smaller than it was.
And yet the very diminution
   makes the smaller dearer.
Just think of gold in nuggets
   sieved from dross or diamonds
   fretted from reluctant coal
   or tons of jasmine under pressure
   lessened to an ounce of ichor.
Let the expanders rant.
They'll learn too late how sunrays –
   focused through a magnifying
   glass into a single, burning
   beam – can re-invent the world.

Documentation

It's all been done: convicted
   wretches tied and torched,
      their hair in flames, their eyeballs
      gone to madness from the pain.
Sliced from diaphragm to groin,
   undead but doomed, the drawn
      and quartered watched their torturers
      spool out their viscera before
      their eyes.
                     Bound missionaries
   fared no better with the squaws,
   who ate their raveled entrails
   as they screamed.
                     The crucified
   died twice – from agony
   and suffocation.
                     A woman punished
   for adultery lost her nose.
Abelard gave up to his castrators
   all that Eloise's father thought
   engendered love, but Abelard
   loved on.
                     And what of her
   whose rapist took her tongue,
   forearms and eyes to keep her
   from identifying her defiler?
The alphabet of cruelty is infinite:
   grandmothers in their eighties
   raped by a platoon and stabbed,
   a traitor buried living
   in a box, a sentenced mutineer

lashed bloody by a cat-o'-nine
before he walked the plank,
Benito Mussolini shot
and hung by the boots like carcass
beef in Piazza Loreto.
Imagine something worse,
    and it's been done, is being
    done or will be done.
"There is nothing one man
    cannot do to another," wrote Carolyn.
In Lebanon and Salvador she saw
    what she would never want
    to know but never could deny.
Unspeakable, of course, but so.

Manolete and Islero

In the Museo Taurino in Córdoba, two rooms preserve the
legacy of Manolete. The first of dark wood is the very
study in which he conducted business. The other encases
or displays his sword, cape, three suits of lights, the
supine graveyard replica of his likeness in effigy and his
last shirt torn and yellowed with fifty-year-old
bloodstains. Stretched and mounted on one wall splays
the black hide of Islero, the bull that gored Manolete to
death while it was being fatally stabbed by him in the last
second of the last act of the last fight of the last tour in
Manolete's career. The hide displaces approximately one
third of all the wall space and dominates the room.
I wonder at this Spanish sense of proportion when I ask
one Spaniard, who, like Manolete himself, is a Cordobés,
why so much space was given to Islero. "Why not?" he
answers. "Look at what he did."

Sex

"Forget the love scenes," he said.
"Which ones?" she answered, "Half
  the movie was one love scene
  after another."
                "I counted five."
She shrugged as if the number
  made no difference, then asked,
  "How many people make love
  on the kitchen table, for God's sake?"
"How would I know?"
                "Besides,
  there's too much showing
  plus all that huffing and puffing."
"I read somewhere that it's like
  nudism – everything displayed,
  nothing revealed."
             "It's insulting
  to women, and I'm a woman."
She poured more coffee in his cup.
He said, "Not much is hidden
  any more."
        "Not *anything.*"
                 "I guess
  you're right."
        "My mother's mother
  never knew a thing until
  her wedding night, but still
  she had six children and was happy."
"I guess she learned as she went."
"What's more – when she was eighty-two
  she still believed adultery was just
  the opposite of infantry."

He laughed
and said, "That shows how men
and women differ where it comes
to sex."
She poured some coffee
for herself and said, "With men
it's all performance."
"What's wrong
with that?"
"Nothing, until they can't."
"Can't what?"
"Just when they get good
at it, they find it harder
and harder to do."
"Let's change
the subject."
"I guess it's just
a case of desire getting ahead
of ability."
"Let's change the subject."

The General

He considers smiling a weakness.
Better to say he's read Sun Tzu,
likes Verdi, has grandchildren
and a twelve-year-old Shih-Tzu.

He strides with the unabridged stance
of a man accustomed to deference.
He plays the courtier with women,
bowing as he kisses their hands.

A rainbow paragraph of battle
ribbons flashes like a flag
above his left breast-pocket.
The stars on his tunic twinkle.

With other generals he sees
himself as equal but detached.
With colonels he parades his rank
like a gander courted by geese.

He says that war makes men,
that men are created for war
no matter where, why or when.
Wait, and he'll say it again.

Accident Ahead

Caboosed behind a funeral
  of truck after truck after truck,
  you edged downhill until
  you passed the relics of bus
  hoods crumpled like excelsior,
  station wagons overturned
  and compact cars compacted
  even more just hours earlier
  and left for scrap.
                    Firemen
  in helmets and hip-high boots
  still browsed the berms.
                      Fire engines
  and an ambulance kept idling in case.
Later a newscaster would claim
  that six of the fifty lives affected
  by the pile-up ceased on impact.
He blamed black ice.
                "It's what
  you never see until it's much
  too late because it fools
  the naked eye."
               That sounded
  too impending to be overlooked.
It spoke to you of more
  than January roads.
                The more
  you drove, the more you saw
  the implications and the risks
  as if you were a target in a hunter's
  sights.

With both hands
tightly on the wheel, you steered
into the unforeseeable and unforeseen
but definite black ice ahead,
beyond and all around you.

Seeing My Mother in My Grandson

Alive, she'd be in her nineties.
Dying on Wilkins Avenue
  and buried from home, she never
  saw forty.
           Six decades back
  I crept downstairs to see her
  coffined in our living room…
Today, through me to my own son
  and through my son to his,
  I'm witness to a resurrection.
                  The baby's
  brows and lashes are hers.
So is the roundness of his face
  and ever so slightly, the smile…
His mother says he has his father's
  features softened by her.
And I agree.
          But I go further
  back, think long and stop short.
Some things are known at sight,
  some not, and some through memory
  and what the heart can never
  quite deny.
          And each
  is wrong.
         And both are right.

On The Stroke of

I

Is life equivalent to digits
  nicked across a gravestone?
Or is it more?
                Or both?
Or neither one?
                Or something
  else entirely?
                At two
  plus fifty Shakespeare was over.
Scholars agree while others
  claim he lives in forty plays,
  a sequence of sonnets, seven
  poems and a handwritten plea
  for money.
                Believers claim
  that Shakespeare lived and wrote
  as God intended.
                Cynics
  say what difference does it make?
The sick still suffer, wars
  keep happening, and everyone
  who dies dies disappointed…
Four views of a single Shakespeare…
Just one of the four is true.

2

If he had gone the day
  before or not at all,
  these words would not exist.

If he had turned one block
   before he turned, nothing
   would have happened.
                              Had he
   but looked, the impact might
   have been avoided.
                              Instead,
   we woke to one less driver
   in the world, a father in grief,
   and a sister and brother bereft.
We said the place and time
   were wrong, but these and all
   the laws of physics worked
   as they should.
                              The traffic lights
   kept flashing red and green
   in sequence.
                              Seated riders
   passed at fifty miles per hour
   in their designated lanes to prove
   that bodies in motion stay
   in motion unless another body
   in motion's in the way.
                              Granted,
   the impact cost one life,
   but the logically lethal laws
   of physics worked to perfection.

3

Why are all sculpted profiles
   on a coin and every printed
   face on every paper currency
   on earth so serious?
                              There's not
   a smiler in the lot.
                              Why does
   "The Star Spangled Banner"
   start and end with a question?
Why are the four months
   from September through December
   two months out of order?
Why not call ceilings nothing
   but inverted floors?
                              What
   are the implications here for money,
   country, time and architecture?
Answers, if they exist or not,
   are not the point.
                              The point
   is why these questions leave
   so many people quietly
   amazed and, after a pause,
   confused and ready to argue.

The View from Above

is false.
                From the fortieth floor
or from the crown of Mt. Ventoux
it makes details invisible
and distance indistinct.
                                We're left
with patterns, lights or woods,
that's all.
                The illusion, I admit,
relieves.
                The moods we feel
aground are different from our moods
aloft.
        On high, we think
we understand why Eiffel aimed
his tower at the sun, why Simon
fasted on his perch to concentrate
on God the more, why Jack
beanstalked his way to heaven.
Later, our sealevel selves
    correct us.
                        They say that we mistook
mere overviews for vision,
impressions for thoughts, plans
for ideas, and sightings through binoculars
for focus…
                Back down
to earth where love is possible
and murder common, and injustice
no surprise, we meet our lives
again.

The meeting is affectionate
despite a certain awkwardness.
And well it should be.
                    When
was it ever easy to return
from soaring up the beanstalk
of an elevator shaft to reach
the heaven of the topmost floor
where nothing happens but the view?

Middlemost

Alone and listening to songs
  from Andalús in Arabic, I drove
  a midnight road I never
  drove before.
               The music kept
  the dark at bay.
             Traffic
  was sparse while songs composed
  a thousand years ago
  seemed somehow to be sung for me,
  just me.
           I felt as chosen
  as I felt the day I lingered
  near the stone altar of Le Thoronet.
The stone changed color in the sun,
  and what was beige turned saffron
  as I watched.
            The walls walled out
  whatever walls wall out and held me
  centered there.
             I thought that all
  of France and Europe were aswirl
  around me like a carousel
  revolving on its core.
             Nothing
  mattered more than being where
  I stood and who I was.
              It left me
  totally myself but more myself,
  if that makes sense.
            For something
  similar, imagine the moods

of people praying or in awe
or hearing the right word spoken
at the right time or reading
the right word written in the right
way.
       Or think of men
enslaved from birth but overnight
set free.
          Before their ransoming
they might have been content
with being slaves for life.
But afterward, never…
                    That's
what the music said to me.

Everything

Snowflakes are flawless only
  as they fall.
              For just that long
  they're equidistantly themselves,
  slanting in silent millions
  on whatever's there.
                        Fallen,
  they turn anonymous in drifts
  that melt their way from slush
  to gutterwater and again to air.
Why do I think of words
  as snowfall?
              Uttered in English,
  French or Japanese, they let
  themselves be heard before
  they vanish in the selfsame air
  that someone somewhere swallowed
  as a breath to say them in the first
  place.
        Of many that are lost
  so few will be remembered.
But of the few the ones
  that last the brightest burn –
  not long and never long enough –
  like words left over from a dream…
After white blusters burst
  as unexpectedly as dreams, the fathers
  frown and ask how much,
  how deep, how long?
                        Their children
  run to taste the snowflakes

on their lips or catch them in midfall.
They're still too young to know
    the beautiful is always brief
    since brevity has made it so.
The most they want is just
    to taste and touch the snow
    before it goes.
                    That's everything.

In the Time of the Tumult of Nations

We thought that the worst was behind us
  in the time of the tumult of nations.
We planned and we saved for the future
  in the time of the tumult of nations.
The crowds in the streets were uneasy
  in the time of the tumult of nations.
We murdered our annual victims
  in the time of the tumult of nations.
We were fined if we smoked in the cities
  in the time of the tumult of nations.
We gave and deducted our givings
  in the time of the tumult of nations.
We kept the bad news from the children
  in the time of the tumult of nations.
We wakened from nightmares with headaches
  in the time of the tumult of nations.
We voted for men we distrusted
  in the time, in the time, in the time,
  in the time of the tumult of nations.

In the time of the tumult of nations
  the ones who were wrong were the loudest.
In the time of the tumult of nations
  the poets were thought to be crazy.
In the time of the tumult of nations
  the President answered no questions.
In the time of the tumult of nations
  protesters were treated like traitors.
In the time of the tumult of nations
  the airports were guarded by soldiers.
In the time of the tumult of nations
  young women kept mace in their purses.

In the time of the tumult of nations
  the rich were exempt in their mansions.
In the time of the tumult of nations
  we waited for trouble to happen.
In the time of the tumult of nations
  we lived for the weekends like children.

Like children we clung to our playthings
  in the time of the tumult of nations.
We huddled in burglar-proof houses
  in the time of the tumult of nations.
We said that the poor had it coming
  in the time of the tumult of nations.
We readied our handguns for trouble
  in the time of the tumult of nations.
We tuned in to war every evening
  in the time of the tumult of nations.
We watched as the bombs burned the cities
  in the time of the tumult of nations.
The name of the game was destruction
  in the time of the tumult of nations.
We knew we were once better people
  in the time of the tumult of nations.
We pretend we are still the same people
  in the time, in the time, in the time,
  in the time of the tumult of nations.

3

Encore, Encore

It's true that I repeat myself,
  but knowingly.
                But so do
  lovers in the very act, and no
  less ardently.
                  Over and over…
The same holds true for us
  each time we eat or drink
  or simply breathe…
                  Some say
  that repetition bores.
                  I say
  it reassures.
           Even our chores
  are gifts of sorts because
  they give us something to do:
  busheling leaves, raising
  a spit-shine on cordovan shoes,
  selecting from a slate of names
  a candidate we loathe the least.
It's always differently the same.
Sometimes a variation brightens
  a chore the way a new
  addition livens a collection.
"The thousandth time may prove
  the charm," wrote Frost, and he
  was right.
           But even Frost
  would say that only repetition
  makes the variation charming.
Meanwhile we keep repeating what
  we do – like heartbeats, like the seasons,

like composers who revive dead themes
and make them sound alive again.
It's always differently the same,
  as I said, as I said, as I said…

At Home

Two decades of hell could not
  convince Odysseus to think
  of Ithaca as just another island.
Where else did Churchill go
  in his defeat but back to what
  he fondly called his "habitation?"
What else but home restores us
  in the wake of acts of God
  or national catastrophes?
Unlocked, an opening door
  extends its own welcome.
Obedient chairs remain on duty
  at attention, and sleeping rugs
  stay territorial as ever.
While clocks repeat their treadmill
  trek of going nowhere
  by the numbers twice a day,
  the furnace hums the only
  tune it knows.
            Later
we find the cardinal that died
  colliding with our kitchen window.
We bury it enfolded softly
  in its wings like every bird
  in death.
        The birch beyond
the driveway tells us why
  our house is not an igloo
  or a hut.
        The gulp of faucet-water
being swallowed by an unplugged
drain in a swirling funnel

mimics the treachery of suckpools
and whirlwinds.
                    If all our books
were people once, we house
a thousand people underneath
one roof.
                    The pause between wars
the world calls peace is not
their peace.
                    They are our truest
natures peacefully in print
in perpetuity.
                    Like bottles of patient
wine they age in place
and wait to share themselves
with anyone.
                    Opened, they seem
the same as doors extending
welcomes, page by page.

For Which It Stands

Crosswinds have slashed the flag
  so that the thirteenth ribbon
  dangles free or coils around
  the flagpole like a stripe.
                    What's left
  keeps fluttering in red-and-white
  defiance.
           Somehow the tattering
  seems apropos.
              The President
  proclaims we'll be at war forever –
  not war for peace but war
  upon war, though hopefully not here.
Believers in eternal re-election
  hear his pitch and pay.
                In Washington
  God's lawyer warns we stand
  at Armageddon, and we battle
  for the Lord.
            Elsewhere, California's
  governor believes in California's
  governor, and football bowls
  are named for Mastercard, Pacific
  Life, Con-Agra and Tostitos.
Out west a plan to gerrymander
  Colorado (Texas-style) fails,
  but barely.
            Asked why no flag
  is studded in his coat lapel
  or decorates his aerial, a veteran
  responds, "I wear my flag
  on my heart – I don't wear

my heart on my sleeve."
                             Today
for once we're spared the names
of occupying soldiers shot
or rocketed to fragments in Iraq.
Collateral damage?
                         Two boys,
their mother and both grandparents.
No names for them…
                           Just Arabs.

The Nearness That Is All

Love's what Shakespeare never
  said by saying, "You have
  bereft me of all words, lady."
Love is the man who siphoned
  phlegm from his ill wife's throat
  three times a day for seven
  years.
      Love's what the Arabs
mean when they bless those
with children: "May God keep them
for you."
      Or why a mother
whispers to her suckling, "May you
bury me."
      Love's how the ten-year
  widow speaks of her buried
  husband in the present tense.
Love lets the man with one leg
  and seven children envy no man
  living and none dead.
          Love
  leaves no one alone but, oh,
  lonely, lonelier, loneliest
  at midnight in another country.
Love is jealousy's mother
  and father.
      Love's how death
creates a different nearness
but kills nothing.
      Love
  makes lovers rise from each
  loving wanting more.

                              Love
        says impossibility's possible
        always.
                    Love saddens glad
        days for no bad reason.
Love gladdens sad days
        for no good reason.
                              Love
        mocks equivalence.
                              Love is.

Paring Pairs of Pears

Anjou, Seckel or Bartlett –
  what's the difference?
                   Potted,
  they boil down from chunks
  to mush, bubbling from pear-wine
  to pear-stew, pear-sauce, all
  the possibilities of pear before
  pear-brittle.
           Why do I think
  of logs afloat and boiled down
  to driftwood by incessant tides?
Of poems boiled into brevity
  through nights and even years
  of afterthought?
             Of all the living,
  even as I write, now boiling
  suddenly or slowly into bone?

Body Language

"How's your headache?" she asked.
"Easing," he answered, "but I'm
   fighting it."
                  "How do you fight
a headache?
                  For us women
pain is pain.
                  If we hurt,
we cry or scream or just
say so."
                  "But that makes pain
the winner."
                  His eyes were strafing
the beach while she kept lotioning
her thighs.
                  They'd been in Cannes
for a week, and all their talk
was anatomical.
                  She blamed this
on the semi-nudes who flanked them
daily on the beach.
                  She said
the women were "mistakenly unclothed."
For him the girl on his right
   was one of hundreds to appraise.
"This goddess beside me," he whispered,
   "is feeling no pain whatsoever."
She glanced at the girl and muttered,
   "Meat with eyes."
                  "To you,
maybe, but she proves the female

body in its prime is beauty
at its best."
                    "We don't stay prime
for long, Josh."
                    "But while
it lasts, you're 'sport for Jove.'"
"All women work the same
    inside, so don't be fooled
    by the wrapper."
                    Quickly she capped
    the lotion bottle with a twist
    and snapped, "You men are boys
    in men's clothing.
                    You love us
    only from the waist down."
"I love you down and up
    plus 'all the demesnes that there
    adjacent lie.'"
                    "Thank you,
    Mercutio."
                    "It's true."
                    "Then, why
    do you leer at the mermaid beside you?"
"Because she's beautiful."
                    "Then what?"
"That's where it ends."
                    "I hate
    to question your aesthetics, Josh,
    but that's where it *starts*," she said
    and stood, "so watch, and I'll show you
    the 'ocular proof.'"

                              With that,
        she turned, shucked off her swimsuit,
        asked him to hold it and posed
        like Cleopatra, Rosalind and Desdemona
        so that he and everyone would see
        how bodily convincing she could be.

My Shirt Inspector Reassures Me

Small as a stamp, his note
   explains that he's "examined every
   detail of this garment to make
   sure it meets our high quality
   standards."
               Not that I asked…
Still, it's comforting to know
   that someone out there named
   Inspector Twelve stands
   for perfection.
              Auto mechanics
   simply send a bill.
               Messengers
   say there's "postage due."
Parking lot attendants
   market space by the half hour
   and make us feel lucky to park.
Not that we balked…
              Although
   a shirt is just a shirt,
   Inspector Twelve impresses me.
All sticklers for details impress me.
They help me see how much
   the often overlooked might be
   what means the most.
               Take science.
Scientists have said that saving
   insects matters more than saving
   whales.
       Rid us of insects
   for a decade, and we're gone.

The principle's the same for those
  who say that life amounts
  to years.
           What about minutes?
Where and when and how
  we live the most and why
  we die go by in minutes,
  more or less.
           With that in mind,
  Inspector Twelve might name
  as mere illusions of arithmetic
  the years we count and call a life.

At Churchill's Grave

Call it the battleship of tombstones,
    but amply deserved, all things
    considered.
                    After the blunder
    at Gallipoli, he turned to soldiering
    and politics and warned of Hitler
    in the interbellum.
                    No one
    listened but Hitler himself.
He balked at bantering with Bevan,
    fearing Bevan's Welsh wizardry
    in argument.
                    Later he wangled
    Stalin's armies to the cause
    in spite of Eisenhower, Roosevelt
    and Charles DeGaulle.
                    Still later
    came that business with the Iron
    Curtain and his hopes for Europe.
No small achievement for a man
    more portly than most who smoked
    cigars, wrote English prose
    so lucidly he won the Nobel
    Prize for Literature and painted
    watercolors in the country when the voters
    turned him out.
                    After he died,
    his widow Clementine, refusing
    all largesse, would sell them,
    one by one, in order to subsist.
Call him a commoner with more
    than common attributes.

"One
of our better sort," the usher said
before the rain smeared all
the carvings on the Bladon tomb
except for
CHURCHILL
over
Winston Leonard Spencer
and the dates.

Tortoise Time

So small, so matched with turf
  he can be taken for a stone
  until he stirs.
              Hunkered
  in his hull like pain, he plods
  on toes of slow-motion feet.
Robins can flock to the tropics,
  swallows return to Capistrano,
  grizzlies snooze in the Yukon,
  and wild rabbits hanker
  for their holes.
              At peace in place
  he comes from where he was
  to where he'll be like afterthought's
  caboose.
          What's distance
  or weather to one whose there
  and here seem always the same?
While rabbits flee, he mimes
  Diogenes beneath his hood
  and sidles forward slower
  than the time of day.
              If home
  is what he is, he's home
  to start with since he never
  goes away.
          Aesop understood.

Towels

What purpose have they but to rub
  skin dry by being drawn behind
  the back two-handed down
  the showered spine or fluffed
  between the thighs and elsewhere?
Yardgoods lack what towels
  proffer in sheer, plump tuft.
Wadded after use and flung
  in hampers to be washed, they clump
  like the tired laundry of men
  who sweat for a living.
                    Spun dry
  or spreadeagled to the sun,
  they teach us what renewal means.
Touch them when they're stacked or racked,
  and what you're touching is abundance
  in waiting.
                    Imprinted with the names
  of Hilton or the Ritz, they daub
  with equal deft the brows
  of bandits or the breasts of queens.
What else did Pilate reach for
  when he washed his hands of Christ
  before the multitudes?
                    Even
  when retired to the afterlife of rags,
  they still can buff the grills
  of Chryslers, Fallingwater's windows
  or important shoes.

                        However
small, it seems they have
their part to play.
                        But then,
en route from use to uselessness,
it's no small asset ever
to be always good at something.

Woman with Walker and Limping Dog

The only beast that "taketh
  to man" precedes her like a little
  horse.
        Or rather a donkey
with downturned eyes, meek
paws and total resignation
to his fate.
          Sixty birthdays
separate them, but in fact
he's just her age.
         They seem
to stand stockstill in motion,
each step at once a comma
and a questionmark.
           With or without
  a leash, they're linked for life.
Day after day, their stroll
  will stay the same, but older.

Lucky

The work I thought I would do
  in the town where I thought I would live
  with the girl I thought that I loved
  was wrong from the start.
                         So much
  for plans and what philosophers call
  choice.
            My work and town
  found me.
              The girl I love
  I met by chance.
                 What made it
  possible was luck.
              For this
  I'll never be grateful enough.
But grateful to whom?
               Something
  as unpredictable as luck has no
  identity.
         Item: Leon and I
  were chatting near first base.
The shortstop's throw was high
  and whistled like a shot between
  our totally distracted heads.
An inch this way or that,
  and one of us would surely
  have been brained.
              The saviour?
                  Luck.
Item: after eleven childless
  years I visited Jamaica

with my wife – I to lecture,
she to shed the flu.
                              Nine
months later, we had a son.
We're still bewildered by the once
    of it, but no less thankful.
The midwife of this marvel?
                                        Luck.
Item: assembling words
    from six and twenty letters
    to be read and understood
    is nothing less than magical.
Who named these letters in the first place?
Who said they stand for sounds
    that Shakespeare quilled and Lincoln
    penned exactly as I'm doing
    now in plain American for you?
Magical.
                    No other explanation.
What makes it happen?
                                Luck.

For Anna Catherine on Thanksgiving

The first girl in generations,
  you came when the century clicked
  from nines to zeroes to plus one.
Capped on a palette, you flexed
  your toes and let us count
  your fingernails.
                  We studied you
  as our particular event,
  our small surprise, our bonus.
Months earlier, I prayed
  that you'd be born intact
  and healthy, and you were.
Today I wish you beauty, grace,
  intelligence – the commonplace
  grandfatherly cliches….
                     What
  makes us crave for those
  we love such bounties of perfection?
Life, just life, is never
  miracle enough no matter
  how we try to church ourselves….
Squirming in my arms, you save me
  from my tyranny of dreams
  with nothing but your version of a kiss
  and the sure, blind love of innocence.

4

A Czech Susannah in Cannes

Supinely tanning at attention
  on her towel, Lefka's beyond
  description.
                    The naked breasts
  of lounging women often lounge
  themselves, their shapes re-shaping
  differently with every turn.
Not Lefka's.
                    Mounding and barely
  pendant, they're peepingly awake.
They match in sepia her swimmer's
  thighs, her sprinter's ankles
  and her navel-centered midriff
  diving to the loins where gold
  triangular lamé protects
  the first and last of privacies.
Her face is all of her
  from eyebrows down to insteps.
Simply by being, she tells us
  that desire's not the same as passion,
  passion but the energy of love,
  and love the silence after ecstasy
  when ecstasy has come and gone.
Like any orchid in its prime,
  she's there to be observed and memorized,
  and so we ogle like the elders.
Watching, we become bewitched.
The more we watch, the more
  we share with France "an enviable
  ease with pleasure."
                    Unease
  awaits us, and we know that in advance.
But now who cares?

                           The sun's
noon-high.
                    The sea seems placid
as a pool.
                    And nothing in the sky's
unclouded distance can distract us
from a girl so beautiful she makes
our daily dread of suffering
or violent death seem suddenly
the stuff of fantasy, not fact.

There's Such a Thing As Lightning

Whatever you expected happened
  differently or not at all,
  but what did happen purely
  by surprise became your life.
That meeting over lunch...
                        Who
  could have guessed a job,
  a princess and a dozen Junes
  in France would come of it?
And that's not all: the winter
  of the fractured tibia that let you
  write a book, the night
  when Archer bested Sugar Ray
  in Robinson's last fight to prove
  that time's the enemy, the years
  Roncalli governed as *"un pape*
  de passage" and changed the world.
Forget "the best-laid plans."
What interrupts the life you plan
  is nothing else but life mistaken
  for an interruption.
                  Pearl Harbor
  was an interruption.
                Meeting
  the blind date who's now
  your wife or waking to the son
  you thought you'd never have
  were interruptions.
                  Earthquakes.
Hurricanes.
      Icebergs.

Miracles.
Jackpots.
Even these words
are interruptions, coming as they do
without announcement or permission.
They're like a group of relatives
you haven't seen in years.
They just
barge in and test your hospitality,
attention, patience and the rest.
They play the role of uninvited
pests pretending to be welcome
guests…
What else is there
to do but make the best of it?

Novembering

The prophesying trees have leafed
  from ripe to amber to maroon
  to khaki.
         Cloudbursts of wrens
  soar southward in flocks.
Mountain by mountain, Pennsylvania
  slows, subdues and closes
  for the season.
            Where is the spell
  of the first crocus, the oak
  that branched from bare to bountiful
  in weeks, the trumpeting lilies
  in their prime?
            If entropy is where
  we're heading, this shutting down
  prefigures it.
         Some say
  it's just a rest and hibernation
  for a flowering to come.
            But death
  is always death, impermanent
  or permanent.
         Today my mood's
  at odds with resurrection.
            Watching
  the wrens, I live the double dream
  of soaring off while staying
  absolutely where I am.

Resoundings

Inside the scalp that gloves
   the skull that shells the brain
   that cups the universe, you hear
   repeated everything you heard.
Not voices only, but the after-
   silence of sung songs,
   of speeches said, of storms
   when all their rain is spent,
   their fusillades of lightning
   banished to the stars, their thunders
   mute as kettle-drums gone dumb.
Even the never heard resounds
   the way that echoes re-invent
   whatever wakened them.
The car says, "Drive me."
The book says, "Read me."
The ball says, "Bounce me."
The fire says, "Fear me."
The bride says, "See me."
The child says, "Hold me."
The tone-deaf listen but never
   hear.
        They think that silence
   is the end of everything,
For them it rhymes with nothing,
   and nothing more will come
   of it.
        You hope your silence says
   that everything will, that everything
   does, that everything did.

Such Stuff

"Death is sovereign over nothing but appearances."
  Guiseppe Ungaretti

It stuns us while we're watching
   tugboats slowly budging
   barges of coal downriver.
Or when the first leaves swirl
   groundward like severed wings.
Shaken, we feel as temporary
   as the wind.
                    We see ourselves
   as ones of millions destined
   for demise by violence or sicknesses
   beyond avoidance.
                         All
   that we did or earned or gained
   translates at once to zero....
Facing the worst he could foresee,
   Camus chose consciousness
   instead of suicide.
                       Sophocles
   rebelled at eighty-eight
   by lifting weights.
                        Nearing
   a hundred, Stanley proclaimed,
    "Imagination keeps us young
   because it's never old and never
   ages."
             And Stanley is right.
Among the fading dreams
   we call appearances, we find
   the only life we can create.

This means we are whatever
  we can make.
               And what we make
  is ours to choose.
               And what
  we choose is how we dream.
Momentary as it seems, we're totally
  our very selves for just
  that long – mortal but permanent.

Crisscross

It can be common as two roads
  slashing through each other
  at right angles in the middle
  of a desert.
                Afterward,
  both roads go on but differently.
Intersecting makes them seem
  more finite, X'ed on the earth
  like a brand of their own making.
What is it stays at the core
  of the cross where the roads collided
  at full speed?
                Is it the force
  of impact crucified forever
  in the vortex?
                Is it a magnet
  in the very eye of north, south, west
  and east?
            It nails us to the axis.
The rest is nothing but mileage.

The Slower the Surer

"Haste is a sign of bad breeding."
   Arab Proverb

Sipping coffee, strolling
   on the Promenade d'Anglais to nowhere
   in particular or listening alone
   to Benny Goodman playing
   Paganini....
                    I savor these
   as slowly as I can to make
   the flavors stick.
                          Though slowness
   lets them linger longer,
   they pass...they pass.
                          This proves
   that all the time between
   the having and the having had
   is everybody's now and then.
Trying to make what's passing
   stay, I tell myself that living
   day by day is good,
   but hour by hour is better,
   and minute by minute is best.
But that's impossible.
                          Since nothing
   slackens on command, I know
   the only slowness that endures
   accompanies its cause: the hesitant
   but noble shame that stirs us
   to apologize, the way a bride
   perfects her wedding look,
   the tardy tinkering that sets

a poem or a painting or a broken
finger straight.
                            Compare this
to the milking of a cow.
                                    Squeeze
quickly or too forcefully, the cow
will lash you with her tail.
Too slowly, and she'll stomp and kick
    the pail.
                    But milked with patience,
she will stand as if asleep and let
herself be eased until her udders
shrivel dry.
                        In just that way
the world that's happening extracts
the same submission for the same
but all too temporary slowness
that is ours to keep just long
enough to know it's passing by.

Passing Through

Bolted to bricks above
  the door of each garage,
  a backboard offers to the neighborhood
  its hoop and net.
               Linked lawns
  flow leisurely as putting greens
  aswirl around their punctuating
  cups.
          Driveways meander
  like private roads to nowhere.
If multiple redundant welcomes
  greet you in blocked letters
  from resplendent welcome mats, ignore
  the duplication.
               The similar bricks,
  the similar footage from the curbs,
  the similar windows and shut doors
  announce that no one's home
  though someone's home.
                 Your eyes
  keep skimming over surfaces
  that rhyme at random to the point
  of boredom.
           Something makes you
  hunger to disrupt the utter
  sameness of it all.
             Something
  craves the rainbow neighborhoods
  of Curaçao, the rock houses
  of Rocquebrune or the thatched roofs
  of Hull where nothing matches
  but the common, customary preference
  that nothing – but nothing – should match.

A New Deal

"Who says we need a new car
  now, right now, today?"
For her a car was transportation,
  nothing more.
                 "This wreck
  burns oil, and the warranty's
  expired."
               "Why not renew it?"
"I want a new car pronto,
  this minute – end of discussion."
It was election day plus one.
The whole country had swung
  to the right.
             He felt betrayed.
"I'll never understand," she said,
  crossing her fingers, "why men
  and cars are just like that."
He drove on automatic pilot,
  tallying the radio returns
  from Maine to Texas through the whole
  catastrophe.
              "Your mind is always
  elsewhere when you drive,
  and that's not safe."
              "The country's
  gone to hell, and all you talk
  about is me, me, me."
"I'm not married to the country."
He turned the radio knob
  a click.
        More tallies, more defeats…

He switched to the golden oldies.
"If you're set on getting a car,
   I hope the color is puce."
"Nobody makes a puce car."
"What about lavender with cream
   appointments?"
                        He looked at her
   as if she'd lost her mind.
Glenn Miller"'s "In the Mood"
   embalmed him in a sulk.
                              For just
   that long he thought of times
   when cars were only black,
   blue or gray, and lavender
   described a sunset or a dress,
   and politics made his kind of sense.
"All right," she said, "I'll take
   apache red with pink leather."
That made him mad enough
   to spit.
              He inched the window
   down, turned halfway to his left
   and spat all over his chin.
Hearing her laugh, he tried
   to stay quite serious.
                              "Not
   funny," he said but found himself
   laughing along with her,
   and neither could stop.

                        Later
they laughed themselves giddy
as drunks each time they brought
it up if politics was in the news
or not.
            They kept the car.

Senior Moments

God, but the numbers mount –
   the executing years, the hours
   pawned for rest, the daily
   razorings, the laughs, the unforeseeables.
The seasons of Ecclesiastes
   wear you down, and all
   for something called longevity.
You've lost your taste for pears,
   for hard salami on rye,
   for sleep, for summering in Cannes
   where everything is nudely shown
   but nothing showing from within.
You blame the change on changing,
   and that's true.
                        But you're the changeling...
   you...just you.
                        You keep
on craving, but the savor's gone.
This brings you back to facts,
   and these divide you into halves.
One half pretends you're what
   you were, and everything is there
   and yours for the enjoying.
The other makes you settle
   for acceptance, compensation, age,
   whatever.
                  But who accepts
   acceptance?
                        And when did resignation
   compensate?
                        The more the past
   is past, the more it re-invents

itself until it's only what
you make of it.
                    Who says
there's more?
                    You're left with watching
the time being turn into the time
been, and who's to stop it?

Mediterranean Update

Whatever let it be a pleasure
  made it end like anything
  that dies before we think
  it should.
           The aisles of lavender,
  the sea "between the land,"
  the houses cut from rock
  where Yeats lived last, the yachts
  moored hull to hull at anchor,
  and the wind from Africa that's known
  as the *libeccio* all blurred
  like painter's pigments fractioned
  into bits.
          "Everything's the same
  but us," I said, "because
  we've come back once too often."
French television flashed
  a raid by F-l6's in Gaza
  followed by a sacrificial bombing
  in Jerusalem.
           The detonated bodies
  sprawled alike.
            "Same intent,"
  I said, "but different weapons."
The prospect made me kick
  aside a core of cardboard
  from a toilet paper roll
  discarded near a dumpster.
             Later
  we paganized ourselves in sun
  and surf – our way of fiddling

while tomorrow burned.
                              Romeos
roamed the beach, sporting
their scrotal pouches.
                              Women
wore nil but thongs and pubic
patches.
              So many thronged
the waves I thought of mullets
or ale-wives surging in frenzy....
Three hours east by air,
    oppressor and oppressed were being
    filmed in battles we would watch
    while dining later in Antibes
    or sipping cappuccino by the pool.

Ballad of All Battles

The first ones to leave were the wealthy.
They packed all they owned and were gone.
Because they were mobile and healthy,
there was nothing to make them stay on.

They left to their fate all the others –
the children, the poor and the lame.
Why bother to see them as brothers
since nobody knew them by name?

The workers remained out of duty.
They called it their city to keep.
Their work had a laborer's beauty,
and their roots in the city were deep.

The bombs made them scatter for cover.
They felt the concussion and prayed.
The few who survived would recover
and number those killed in the raid.

It scarcely concerned the destroyers
to defend what they ordered in haste.
They spoke like disinterested lawyers,
and the dead were collateral waste.

Under siege from all sides but unbeaten,
the starving ate dogs and then cats.
When the last of the cats had been eaten,
the desperate feasted on rats.

Even now who can answer what ended
or even what started the war?
The people were left undefended,
and the innocent died by the score.

Do You Read Me?

It's what communicators ask
  to learn if they are being
understood.
                    Because to read
means more than seeing or hearing,
the verb reverberates.
                    Lovers
read each other's eyes
as clearly as they read their bodies
with a touch.
                    Blind people read
the Braille of chairs and tables
like a book.
                    Mariners read
the sea.
          Forecasters read
the sky.
          The curious read
X-rays, maps and tea-leaves
for solutions.
                    Writing means
reading the passing world
the way a sculptor reads
the body of the model he's remembering
in stone.
          Do you read me?

5

Academia Supremia Anemia

In Academia Supremia Anemia
  the Chairperson says, "We're not
  teaching students to sit and read
  poems under the trees."
                           Shakespeare
  tells him, prithee, to shut up.
The students cheer for Shakespeare.
"Deconstruct constructions now,"
  proclaims the critic.
                     Wordworth
  warns, "We murder to dissect."
To prove his point, he separates
  one tulip into stamen, petals,
  stem and roots, then offers
  not the whole that once exceeded
  all its parts but one dead tulip.
The chancellor exhorts the faculty
  to "total quality performance
  with every class computerized."
Socrates sleeps through his speech
  while Christ's too busy arguing
  the sacred once of everyone
  to hear a word.
                  Since both
  lack terminal degrees, they teach
  remedial courses as substitutes
  or adjuncts at less than minimum
  wage.
           Enter the Director
  of Athletics.
                 He's proud of victories
  but says without conviction

that losses are part of the game.
Emerson suggests he read
  again his essay on compensation.
The DA says, "I know
  that compensation is important,
  but money isn't everything."
Emerson comments no further.
The class president urges
  the graduates to be successful
  people.
        "Successful people,"
  whispers the class clown,
  "or truly successful as people?"
The president, on whom such subtlety
  is lost, ignores the comment.
Three millionaires, one socialite
  alumna and a talk-show host
  are honored with degrees and hoods.
The alumna speaks of loyalty
  and leads the student in the Alma
  Mater.
        No one knows the words.
By the time she stops, Montaigne
  has long since left, followed
  by Dante, Catherine de Medici,
  Pascal, Euripides, Mark Twain
  and some who feign acute
  dyspepsia or urinary urgency.

Going with the Flow

Asked how or when she'd wish
  to die, Eva Marie responded,
  "Quickly, but not today."
On the scale of apt retorts
  that ranks quite high.
                  It makes
  the unforeseen less daunting,
  less horrific.
               DeGaulle
considered growing old
a "shipwreck," but he erred.
Though each of us would like
  to die young when we're as old
  as possible, nobody dies
  of age.
          Something grimmer
  awaits us.
           The final
  executioners are violence
  or some disease.
             Graveyards
  of warbones make the case
  for violence.
          Diseases reap
  the rest.
         Facing these Medusas,
  we turn to stone.
           We stare.
Remembering the given days
  we've lived, we seem to breathe
  like solitary oarsmen on a river.

Seated backward rowing
  forward, we pull with the current.
Even when we sleep our oars,
  the boat keels on as if
  it knows our destination
  in advance.
              And it does...
The river runs and wins.

Seesaws

The bigger the tomb, the smaller the man.
The weaker the case, the thicker the brief.
The deeper the pain, the older the wound.
The graver the loss, the dryer the tears.

The truer the shot, the slower the aim.
The quicker the kiss, the sweeter the taste.
The viler the crime, the vaguer the guilt.
The louder the price, the cheaper the ring.

The higher the climb, the sheerer the slide.
The steeper the odds, the shrewder the bet.
The rarer the chance, the brasher the risk.
The colder the snow, the greener the spring.

The braver the bull, the wiser the cape.
The shorter the joke, the surer the laugh.
The sadder the tale, the dearer the joy.
The longer the life, the briefer the years.

Hugh

Confronting him two decades later
  on the Cape, I hated having
  come.
        "When clergymen retire,"
  he had told me, "best they move
  away."
        Ruddy, fit
  and sixty-five, he did just that
  until I found him lodged
  in quarters offered gratis
  by a friend who cared for him.
It hurt to see him soiled
  on a soiled sofa, dribbling
  coughs of spittle on his chin
  and asking who I was
  and why I came.
           Reminding
  him meant nothing.
            All
  he recalled was the chapel he named
  and the school he built with a million
  pledged by the first parishioner
  he asked.
        He was low church.
"We'd rather be right than call
  ourselves infallible," he'd gibe
  with an Anglican grin.
           Preaching
  or piloting his Thunderbird convertible,
  he wore his collar lightly.

Babbling in a backroom flat
  was how I left him, and the scene
  still stings...
           His obit missed
  the mountain-climbing, bishop-
  baiting, Massachusetts-ranting
  redhead that he was.
                Dying
  in peace was not his suit.
I learned he crowed his cranky
  counsels to the last, let loose
  a Yankee laugh and thundered off.

"Wanted: Meaningful Overnight Partner"

Bumperstickered on the tailgate
  of a truck, it speaks in straight
  evasiveness – polite, complete
  and one-dimensional.
                 For sexually
  active and consensual adults,
  one night might seem too brief
   for dialogue, relationship, encounter.
For those allergic to commitment,
  it's enough.
            For female persons
  who object when male persons
  regard them only as objects,
  overnight or otherwise, it's hardly
  meaningful at all.
               For the chronically
  judgmental or partner-impaired,
  it's double-talk for one-night stand.
Or shacking up.
          For any
  other hidden meanings,
  ask the driver of the truck.

Amazement This Way Lies

You who sacrificed both legs
   in Vietnam and learned to wheelchair
   backward down a flight of stairs
   by clamping handrails in your armpit
   and leaving the descent to gravity,
   and you who gave me back
   the watch my father gave you
   after World War I because
   he saw you needed one for work,
   and you who drank but never missed
   a class and gave your students
   everything that money never could,
   and you who saved me from the worst
   of sufferings, I see you all as dancers.
Offstage, all dancers lounge
   like pitchers between innings.
                              Saving
   their bodies for the dance is half
   the dance.
                  Like barreling down
   stairs or knowing when it's time
   or teaching sophomores or warning
   of the worst, the dance is all.
That's why I'm totally at peace
   when excellence is never forced
   or when what's done is done
   for no reward except the deed
   itself.
              I saw it when Madame
   Lacoste acknowledged each
   well-wisher on her hundredth.

Seated stately as a queen,
  she thanked and took each wisher
  by the hand to leave him
  doubly grateful for the taking.
It's all one dance, you see,
  and watching her was like awakening
  to witness something like a miracle
  one hundred birthdays in the making.

RSVP

"Sophie," he called, "let's go."
She'd planned the whole event
  for months in secret: banquet
  reservations for classmates of his
  from sixty years ago,
  a special cake with eighty
  candles.
            "Sophie, it's late!"
To keep it a surprise the guests
  were sworn to silence.
                        Knowing
  he hated birthday parties,
  she described it as a private
  dinner with a few, close friends.
"Why do I need a dinner
  for everyone to know how old
  I am?"
            "Do it for me."
"You're three years younger."
"So what?"
                "You don't know
  how it feels."
                Such arguments
  went on for weeks, and twice
  he totally refused to go.
"Do it for me," she pleaded.
"Why should I do it for you?"
"Because I asked you, Abe."
                        "Don't
  ask me."
            The secret burst
  when the caterer called while Sophie
  was shopping.

Abe answered
the phone, listened and gasped,
"Two hundred responses for what?"
He waited and snapped, "I don't care
how many guarantees you need!"
Later she had to tell him
everything.
"You mean Morris
is coming from Alaska – and Irv
and Dave, I thought they were dead."
"Everyone who's not dead is coming."
"My God, from Alaska!"
From then
until the final minutes
he took charge.
"Sophie,
for God's sake, hurry up!"
She took deep breaths to calm
herself, cologned her wrists
and hoped that there was nothing
she forgot.
"Sophie, we can"t
be late for something like this!"
Finally, she marched downstairs,
her gown not quite adjusted
and her lipstick still unblotted.
"It's about time," he huffed.
"You," she muttered as she passed,
"I'm not talking to you."

Facing Winter

Robins have fled the suburbs
  for Miami.
               Salt-trucks are set
  to sprinkle safety, street
  by street.
               The leaves have vanished
  into vanished smoke, and houses
  by the hundreds hunker down
  like wagontrains.
               And so do we.
Is it some old fidelity
  that says to change one's weather-zones
  is tantamount to changing one's religion,
  name or looks?
               Who cares
  if we December on a beach
  or flaunt a tanner epidermis
  to the world?
               And who believes
  that staying home deprives us
  of one inch of human dignity?
Returning from a week or so
  of sun will sentence us to opening
  unopened mail, retrieving
  our recorded messages, re-scheduling
  deliveries and testing the utilities
  to see what's working and what's not.
Why not just leave the sunburned
  to their ointments while we scarf and button up
  to face what's inescapable as death
  or age?

Renewable as trees,
we'll learn through weathering that Spring
or its equivalent will always dawn
the dearer and the greener when it's earned.

The Situation

Very well, the news as usual
  is nine-tenths bad.
                       Despite
  a reckless war with random
  deaths, the stock market rallies,
  proving that greed, like fornication,
  battens in bad times.
                       Of course,
  we're not surprised since most
  professions are created by deficiency:
  law from misbehavior, medicine
  from illness, schooling from ignorance.
But does it truly matter?
We try to look ahead, but why?
The worst is always worse
  than we imagined it would be.
No matter what the prophets say,
  they're wrong.
                Even weather
  mocks *The Farmer's Almanac*.
Meanwhile, distractions by the tens
  of thousands vie for our attention
  every day.
             We're just the markets
  or the targets, take your pick.
But while we pick, there's butter
  to be bought, pajamas to be laundered,
  bills to be paid, and news reports
  to be believed or disbelieved.
It's tiring work.
             What is all this

to those who re-create the world
by making or re-making it by hand?
With what's material as wood
or cloth or stone, or immaterial
as words or sounds, they do
what must be done each time
as perfectly as possible and always
with the same respect because
there's nothing truer they can do.

None But The Brazen

Their spear-tips dare a doomed
    inch skyward – doomed because
    of frost predicted for tonight.
You'd like to warn the tulips
    that it's March, not May.
On second thought, why fret?
When did the threat of doom
    deter the merest life from living
    to the fullest?
                    Tulips may die
    tonight, but now they live....
For us the analogues of frost
    are violence, disaster or disease.
Meanwhile we take our chances,
    hoping the end is quick
    but not completely a surprise.
The lingerers persist because
    they have no choice.
                    Babe Ruth
    remained Babe Ruth at less
    than ninety pounds.
                    Bloated
    by cortisone, Georges Pompidou
    warned hecklers not to touch
    the person of the President of France.
Saroyan uttered as his final words,
    "What's next?"
                    Dissimilar, each one,
    but, tulip-like, the same, the same.

What's Left

After we caviled by phone,
  I re-opened your book and read it,
  back to front.
              "My corner
of New Mexico is rather
remote," you told me, as if
remoteness were a fault.
                  Your book
  made caviling forgettable.
Each poem said the unremote,
  redeemable world is all
  we have this side of promises
  we hope are true...
              And if
  they're not, aren't we the better
  for believing?
              Lately I've found
  that most religions just
  repeat themselves.
              Miracles,
  stigmata, uncorrupted corpses
  and the like deliver me to mere
  astonishment but little more.
My counterparts for what you saw
  in your three children or the buffalo
  that almost trampled you to death
  are my grandchildren, Pennsylvania
  and my daily tug-of-war with words.
They never capture fully
  what I know: how children are
  the very clock of life and death

or why my wife's brother's painless
passing saddens and maddens
all that gladdens me or where,
in Wilder's words, we find
the life we lose in living.
No theologian but disturbingly frank,
  Sinatra praised, "Whatever
gets you through the night."
                         What
gets me through the night's no less
a miracle than the slow mercy
of sleep.
           That gift, along with sight,
mobility and what disposes us
to love, is miracle enough.
As for finality?
                Who knows finality
before it happens?
                Meanwhile
the passing present and the past
that's never past are all
that's left.
           And the world is what
you say it is – "not our mother
but a wild music beyond the self."

For Rebecca Seiferle

The Necessary Brevity of Pleasures

Prolonged, they slacken into pain
  or sadness in accordance with the law
  of apples.
                One apple satisfies.
Two apples cloy.
                Three apples
  glut.
        Call it a tug-of-war
  between enough and more
  than enough, between sufficiency
  and greed, between the stay-at-homers
  and globe-trotting see-the-worlders.
Like lovers seeking heaven in excess,
  the hopelessly insatiable forget
  how passion sharpens appetites
  that gross indulgence numbs.
Result?
        The haves have not
  what all the have-nots have
  since much of having is the need
  to have.
                Even my dog
  knows that – and more than that.
He slumbers in a moon of sunlight,
  scratches his twitches and itches
  in measure, savors every bite
  of grub with equal gratitude
  and stays determinedly in place
  unless what's suddenly exciting
  happens.
                Viewing mere change
  as threatening, he relishes a few

undoubtable and proven pleasures
to enjoy each day in sequence
and with canine moderation.
They're there for him in waiting,
and he never wears them out.

To Be

It's time we said that time
   is not the sum of birthdays
   nor how soon it takes to come
   from anywhere to now.
                              No
   longer who we used to be,
   what are we finally but who
   we are?
              After we're gone,
   we live again in those
   we touched.
                    The more we shared,
   the more we had to share
   by giving back tenfold
   what other givers gave us.
It made us similar as songs
   we heard along the way
   and loved so much we learned
   the songs by heart.
                        We came
   to know them as we know
   by heart our very selves.
Those are the songs that save us.